*Selected Poems 1970-2005*

For Catherine, on
a most delightful
encounter.

Elaine
Feb 2006.

Also by Elaine Randell:

*Songs of Hesperus*
*Telegrams from the Midnight Country*
*Untitled*
*Seven Poems*
*A Taper to the Outward Roome*
*Early in My Life*
*Long Hair for Birds*
*This, Our Frailty*
*Larger Breath of All Things*
*Hard to Place*
*Songs for the Sleepless*
*Beyond All Other: Poems 1970-1986*
*Prospect into Breath*
*Gut Reaction*

# Elaine Randell

## Selected Poems
### 1970-2005

Shearsman Books
Exeter

Published in the United Kingdom in 2006 by
Shearsman Books Ltd
58 Velwell Road
Exeter EX4 4LD

ISBN-10 0-907562-71-X

ISBN-13 978-0-907562-71-9

Copyright © Elaine Randell, 2006.

The right of Elaine Randell to be identified as the author of this work has been asserted by her in accordance with the Copyrights, Designs and Patents Act of 1988. All rights reserved. No part of this publication may be reproduced, stored in a retrieval system, transmitted in any form or by any means, electronic, mechanical, photocopying, recording or otherwise, without the prior permission of the publisher.

## Acknowledgements

Some parts of this work have previously appeared in the following volumes: *A Taper to the Outward Roome* (Laundering Room Press, Newcastle-upon-Tyne); *Telegrams from the Midnight Country* (Blacksuede Boot Press, Sidcup); *Early in My Life* (Permanent Press, London & New York); *Larger Breath of All Things* (Spectacular Diseases, Peterborough); *Songs for the Sleepless* (Pig Press, Durham); *Beyond All Other* (Pig Press, Durham). Thanks to all the publishers for their support over the years.

'Against the Air' previously appeared in *The Star You Steer by: Basil Bunting and British Modernism*, edited by James McGonigal and Richard Price. 'Hard to Place' was written while working for "Children Need Families", a project of The Children's Society which places children with special needs into adoptive families.

The publisher gratefully acknowledges financial assistance from Arts Council England.

## Contents

| | |
|---|---|
| Poem: *I look at my two hands* | 9 |
| "It weighed more than I" | 10 |
| More than | 11 |
| "The hen can hatch her eggs . . ." | 12 |
| Upon Watching An Upright Leaf | 13 |
| "When you're lost in the rain" | 14 |
| Songs of Hesperus | 15 |
| Songs of Astraea | 19 |
| In relation to | 21 |
| Park | 22 |
| Song For Each Man In Rain | 23 |
| Too late | 24 |
| Three Poems | 25 |
| Early in my life | 27 |
| As if | 28 |
| Seven Poems | 29 |
| Routine | 31 |
| Suddenly it becomes sordid | 32 |
| Until the gardens are drenched with rain | 33 |
| Covering poem for a letter | 34 |
| Untitled | 35 |
| Watching Women With Children | 36 |
| "A Flame In The Darkness Is The Pilot Of My Loss" | 42 |
| Whether she could take his arm | 43 |
| Drought 1976 | 44 |
| "Which is neither mine nor his but in common" | 45 |
| This time of year | 46 |
| Distant Tender | 47 |
| "Tell them how easy love is" | 48 |
| Waking up in America | 49 |
| Case Note | 50 |
| I prepare myself for the sight of myself | 51 |
| Open Letter | 52 |
| To see who you might be | 55 |
| I am touched by your fear | 56 |
| On sighting the first bluebell | 57 |

| | |
|---|---|
| Dusting | 58 |
| Bitten by it we conjure by touch | 59 |
| This restlessness: this ache | 60 |
| This, our frailty | 61 |
| Diary of a Working Man | 62 |
| After USA | 67 |
| Something you can recognise | 68 |
| Six Pieces from The Sauna | 69 |
| "A soft weeping like rain drumming on dry soil" | 72 |
| Ownership | 73 |
| Collecting sheets | 76 |
| It's very often not who you are but whose you are | 77 |
| *from* Hard To Place | 78 |
| Raising You At Night | 82 |
| The Snoad Hill Poems | 83 |
| Notes one two | 88 |
| "And show myself and everyone as we are . . ." | 89 |
| Beyond All Other | 90 |
| Songs for the Sleepless | 91 |
| If You Have to Push It May Not Fit | 115 |
| We Must Learn Not To Breathe | 116 |
| Kent | 117 |
| This belonging, this us | 118 |
| "Men Must Live and Create. Live to the Point of Tears." | 119 |
| "Who takes the Child By the Hand Takes the Mother By the Heart" | 120 |
| The Path Between the Yew Trees With Grass and Damp With Dew | 121 |
| The Shape of Things | 123 |
| It's Easier Now | 124 |
| Run Down | 126 |
| The Garden | 127 |
| After the Hurricane | 128 |
| Not What You'd Call a Religious Man | 129 |
| I Said Hold Tight | 130 |
| (Untitled) | 132 |
| In Revenge of Civil Disorder | 133 |
| Against the Air | 135 |
| Along the Landings | 136 |

This book is dedicated to the memory of my mum, Daphne Randell (1927-2005), whose love, encouragement, humour and realism stood me in good stead.

It is also dedicated to my husband Ian, daughters Phoebe, Beatrice and Naomi, and to my friends, with love.

## Poem

I look at my two hands
the complete strata.
Capable of it all
& to be
is surely without
dull clap of sound
or another rude awakening
to the bud.
And now it's already yesterday.
As if
I was nothing but the
wood to which
the bow is strung.
Flowers
are buds
turned inside out.

## "It weighed more than I"

who taps to glance at
thread and wave love as if it
were a certain emblem.
Trees are our silver
from the window I watch
bodies lean forward against the hail/We are
wind and bright blue.
The field is dark
& draws skin taut to
flesh/ An old man walks
out of the door to stand.
He cannot think why he came.

## More than

stars perpetuate silver.
Belief.
Yet not enough
we make demand to
trouble air
contend with nothing.
Delight
simple
as catching your face
half turned toward
street light.
The heart is a trellis work
of many.
I would not walk away now.
The tree astounds my
prospect into breath.

> *"The hen can hatch her eggs because her heart is always listening"*

Tend the human frame,
touch dangerously in
the quiet street of patience.
People and animals die in winter
their old arms rise
according to the state of cloud
        the easy bay of horizon.
Constant tilling ear of this age
covers the world with pollen.
Pull the heart into shelter
for we can barely limp back into
the yard our heads bowed in relief of tears.

## Upon Watching An Upright Leaf

If I seem to have come this far
without pausing
its not for lack of exercise that
love extends its bugle
to play the Tarantella.
I sit here, able as an echo
walking home, evening squeezes
my arm.
Consider the lilies.

How I demand time to be my schooner
for the river to approach to be
scalded into the hour and kiss
of forever. At ground level
the trees can only get greener,
the light rain feeds Buttercups
who shrug at us in their yellow hats.
Birds fly up in series against all
who dare to curse this.
Nothing can possibly clash.
The gull its sea.
The Wrapper its Street.
The Sun its Moon.

## "When you're lost in the rain"

A need to be rocked forever and assured
in the warm sleeve of love.
The pavement could be any mans blues
that some misdemeanour throws up to
land between the smudge of self and
myth of the Redwood.
Outside the slow clime of the street acrobats plausible smile
as though
all mankind were as alone as the
events and hours that sway him
into the compulsion of love.

## Songs Of Hesperus

### I

This is like sitting
in a railway tunnel.
"what is this phantom
of the mind
This love, when sifted
and refined?"
All birds in a patient forest
are mute - This
room is full of rocks
and if there's any choice
left I'll take the white.
This man has vision for two.

### II

Voice
Eyes
Longing hands
Weeping trees
in tremble.

### III

We swallow earth
It is a warm room.
How do you ask a
carrier pigeon to return?
Leaves fall

I have almost
lived a season with you.
We graze too much
(in passing)
to recover.

    IV

  Soon.
  Without
  what need to
  rattle on.

    V

    This morning
I am sweet Poll of Plymouth
"And have they torn my love away"
Crimson apples grow on the tree
        next door.
It is twenty degrees above
        laughter
    in this keyhole.

    VI

    Spirits melt.
Why is this square always
     so holy

      I read your letter
      I read your letter
      I read your letter
      I read your letter
What is this strange procession
    of animals.
There aren't many saints left
    to talk to.


### VII

You are going home.
I wonder how you lie at night.


### VIII

          – there are no trees
left in the North Sea    now
just this
        splintered sun
and human loss.
There is so much salt
        stretched.
Sweet bliss   (gulls)
pump wings – there is a tired pain
in his heart
Loss.

We too fly home alone.

## IX

Bells sang out of the blue sky
Trees burst
Heaven now seems lighter.
This night holds
no scream
just the tap
as you approach
come
as a tetrachord.

As a letter unsounded – silent.


## X

To reach the top
you've got to climb.
Soft grief.
Chime.
Stratum of tree.

## Songs of Astraea

I

Strike in the nest
reek into a certain pool.
How do you seal the
corners of the heart?
A wheelbarrow stands full
of cut grass.
Lip to lip, breath to breath
we divide the zealous,
confirm the boring.
Outside this blown semaphore
night – (if I should fail
tell me ) – it's more than
travelling it's like living
inside your magnificent airplane
heart.


II

"If I could sing of only one
song. I'd sing of you"
Perhaps tonight in the high
brick tower you are wounded.
Morning – a bird was born in
the eaves of my house;
I heard its new wings move
in folds against
the peep of day.

III

Like Midas you waited
to lick life into the
branches;
help a trapped Salmon
to his river.
This evening I wept for
you – with joy of walking
through leaves.


IV

Only the sacring bell
heliostat for breath
    in the
 dark blue woodland.
Carry this heart around
the batteries won't fade.
I shall not make the morning
   without you.


V

Of you
being
the father
to my child
the songster in the
woodshed,
sower of seed, vein
of leaf,
Message of Sepal.

## In relation to

the wet face of the world
many
kindnesses we remember. Ever
y woman walks around. This
onus populus.

Important.
Sudden cold.
Eternity spits on our new shoes.
Refuge of each bulb.
A house would not hold us
its hard outer lips strut
no one would travel to see it.

The radio is still/ it
plays while
you stand at the window to watch local
bird life.
Another jerky film from Asia.
We all go home
and talk about each other.

## Park

light behind two dozen trees.
Bear bounty of notion.
A fine life of the painter
his hard shirt of frozen bleached
mild dew.
Vacant park
the only thing we may leave intact.
That shrapnel of independence
we find will not hold air.
(Certainty barks us hollow limb from bough)
Imitate sap.
No
thing can be dis grace full, it is all as agile
as it seems.
Earn every survival.
Frequent the treasure to hold this
your utter love.

## Song For Each Man In Rain

Tread the continuously perfect
smell of wet grass – how easy
it has all become.

Always corrugated roofing.
Children inside school. Come
to believe in what we know most of.

Verse is a bull of the lunatic,
this natural rim of the kingdom.
Applaud life and birds.

Allow everything to wander
Find each still item beneath its
quiet crisis.

He walks back again and again past the house
kicks at damp earth.
Waste the heart out over gravel.
The clouds reassemble like orphans.

## Too late

for stars
and barefoot I return home.
Growing pains.
The trees are covering the street lights,
my hand on the far side of your wrist
and all that withstands pain.
People in bus queues, they lean and sway
and put down bags and take them up again.
Death steals us back.
And tonight someone is whistling as they
walk along the pavement
is taking stride after stride with air in
their lungs
is wearing clothes that fit and move
is carrying objects dear to them
is walking home never the same again.

## Three Poems

1

Heart overbeating
I pace tired ground
move to light tears
and heady distraction
by the look of a woman
carrying bags standing
in a doorway
some miles
from here
her bent hand
resting as it did
on her forehead
if only for that
I am waiting.


2

Trying to build homes
rain soaked women
walk the High Street carrying lino
       prepacked vegetables
       bread.
Rain on every inch until after five
when the men with long strips of wood
corner home together.
In the graveyard opposite
two children up to their thighs
in long grass
on the street a woman walks by in
lace hat and gloves.

3

There are fingerprints
on the glass of the television
shop where the men stand around
watching cricket at lunch time
and the women wander past in jeans
and light weight rain coats with
midweek shopping.
The bus crews come out of the pub
red faced and argue. Another hardware
sale in the High Street selling chrome
taps and fittings.

# Early in my life

So we
are left with action
that device we only know the
carriage of.
The clouds reiterate.
I give up the chase.
Late love   early in my life,
pressing as it does leaving me
exquisite fine shadow of hair
the rush of wet road
daily life despite this.
Skilled storage, shelving
of obligation and all too often
the night goes on by and girls
hover in doorways with tattoos –
O rain damaged heart.
The shadow passes over itself
Dark hot evening a dog barking,
church bells.
These;
cliffs we drown upon,
your arms unfelt.

## As if

As if
it were given
night appeals
if only to lone sleepers

non sleepers

who worry the sky
and are caught between
bright tragedy
and taut mornings.

Dark sleep
the lightest mist
on your arm
as it rests
among a spate of aloof
birds where suburban streets
become alive
with an appeal of night

and lone sleepers
non sleepers

who worry within a tearing
that is available to early
dawn birds alone.

## Seven Poems

Only a handful of leaves
left on the tree    and here
listening to the flux
inside the white night


Stave spread on glass
Mercury of a cooling pearl


A crippling in the gore
where the seams of the heart
make a join in the raft
– and its back home –
Tall as a bear in the Sierra
and we learn the steel gauge of
the head
I watch you often
still in the nest
between lip and teat
and the stars make good on your brow


Brush the willow

A spreading acorn
in the chestnut of the breast



Grapple in Lilac
down along
beside the vital
stream under the walls



Lilt over the sway
by the bridge and the elemental lesson
"the space between three violins"
The child with the heavenly
document in the back pocket
of his jeans.

## Routine
*for my mother*

How many times my hands
go to the sink
performing some duty
of the house.
Fingers stretched
       related
           stern, promised.
"take my floured hands
in your entire step"
And if I ask for constancy in my life
do I really suggest solidarity
or boredom or the ability
to learn the agility of others faith
in me.
Too often I am glib with the grief of others,
        I am a creature of flight and earnest
I make my life a belly of people
worn by routine
     by the consistence of stars.

## Suddenly it becomes sordid

Suddenly it becomes sordid
the way death
brings itself onto itself

The queueing people
prepare for the unexpected,
reiterate their good intentions.
Coaches filled with workers from the pit
laugh and climb down in the cages
to the coalface.

Suddenly it becomes sordid
as if I could do nothing
but watch heavy eyed and turn away.
Women meet one another in the street
and laugh at their broken hearts and scuffed shoes.
Later they talk about each other and compare crises.

Suddenly it becomes sordid
to argue over what the dead have said
to consider that barter between life and death.

The pink chestnut blossom is here
by the window
– simply it shouts.
How could we be left with ashes of the dead
to fertilise what remains
but we are and how sordid the taste
is any wind that ruffles our smallest preparation.

## Until the gardens are drenched with rain

Alarmed
Disarmed
by light
vulnerable
I have seen you
misty wet
misty wet
with rain.
You watched
from the window.
There is nothing
but the air
the very air
the sea going vessels,
the early tourist,
field upon field
ploughed, levelled, waiting.

## Covering poem – for a letter

I would be
always ready to accept
that you
were too busy to write
or to phone.
I would never
consider making demands
or suggest that we
take a few hours together
or sit with the sun on our backs.
Always the way
it seemed
the possibilities, the speculation.
   O the idea of it would leave us
the skeleton of a day.
You see my dear
I am forever welcoming
forever
out of danger.

# Untitled

Our feet work the sallow
earth
is a changeling is a message
is something to contend with
brought
here on saline brow
lines crease up the whole idea
of it
as something more simple than watching
heat rising in the shadow
contagious field
let me in.

# Watching Women With Children

1.
Wood (and all else) by the sink.
Frozen winter clothes
moss on the path outside,
her veined life.
"Will you know me tomorrow like this?"
lines on her chapped hands
the storm of yesterday.


2.
The day
she woke early
bright sharp dawn.
Eyes that broke the floor
with anger spilled at the child the night before.
"The prism of mere life is unbearable,
plants and animals in their secular change,
eaten up with will power.


3.
The faun of winter has attended with sorrow
concrete and iron steps from the basement
– you could fall so easily –
she thought watching the child totter and smile as she
held out her hand.

4.
His quick tears
swift as a balanced balloonist.
He cried bitterly – heard their shout
and anguish from between the banisters.
Ajax on the flannel and all over the
bathroom floor.
Life, it is known of love
so roughly tested and beaten across
the table.


5.
Woke to find him stirring beside her,
his slight warm body had crept
in early light.
He who turns to look at moon and
name it space beyond all other value
to draw back the curtains and smile at
the stellar desire so gently regarded
as time.


6.
Often walking across
the green square
she would pull the Oak towards her
and they would feed the ducks,
wander home by the library
intent as the hospital steps where
she first heard him cry.

7.
Cleaning the offices
her stern legs
and tired arms    men stand around
in their shoes watching tightly guilty.
She met him from school
by the wire mesh gate.
He ran out, the last child.
"I wet my pants" he cried so hard.
Picked him up, the cold air and his wounds
whipping her heart.


8.
They are laughing together at the back
of an old distant photograph.
A key at the door, he is home,
anxiously worn,
snapping at her for some small mistake.
Shipwrecked we are on so faint a seizure
of reality.


9.
He caught her hand.
The weather, time of year, youth
and its ready soul
– how her Mother had laughed when
later she told him she would not see
him again as he'd almost a limp he'd
received as a boy in the Blitz.

10.
"Seed Propagation" – the teacher told him
to underline it and read aloud from the book.
"Birds are responsible for a great many seeds, they
carry them in their beaks and feathers and drop
them as they pass." He ran into the playground
kicking at a tennis ball.
'Come in right now' the teacher called from the
window 'come along quickly' he ran, his heart
sinking, she had found the torn book.
'It's your Mother' she said 'she's not very well.
Now I'll take you home to your Dad.'
He was not certain of tears, put his coat on and
the teacher did not mention the absence of his cap.


11.
'As if pulled and gripped by pliers
the spine is severed and tortured, the
blood comes and the womb is drained.'
We're going to save your baby – the nurse had said.
But she knew it was helpless,
felt the warm pulse slide between her legs.


12.
Maternal scream
spirit of Eithia damned into salt
unable shadow of trees.
Dreary the belly of cold sheep
scream of even air.
Death whips us from each other
long before we are ready. Hot iced sleep.

39

13.
Cut grass, creosote, tar and urine
in the phone box. She called him.
"I am barren, sterile, empty. My heart has
broken like a Robins egg. This wreck and
all unborn reach the horizon of all finite tears."



14.
"What are you doing?"
'I am listening to the moist cave where all
things begin.'



15.
Along the High Street a woman slaps
her child. Livid at sound.
The lonely assault struck her ribs with clay:
heart broken as a Robins egg.



16.
Leap, don't jump.
They caught her by the coat.
Dangling
moth
like
eighteen storeys up, clothes
limply between the legs.
Shopping list falling from a pocket.

17.
"Hello Mum, I'm home."
He ran into the house.
"Yes, I can see that" she said leaning
away as he tried to kiss her.
"You haven't a cold have you, we don't want
anything spreading."
He ran out into the garden as far
as the lawn would allow.


18.
"The fate of the world today depends
on the common understanding by the
whole human race of what a human being
really is and on enlarging the common notion of
man."

## "A Flame In The Darkness Is The Pilot Of My Loss"

The improbability of chance!
A songflul thrush in the garden.
Your mothers death dips its already bent head
onto our shoulders.
>We cannot talk of it now
>and speak in whispers
>waiting, so grief may find
>its cleaner way.
"Love, faith and flesh alone"
We will not forget.
In the playground the children have left
a clean handkerchief
folded on the tarmac.

## Whether she could take his arm

and hold it casually so close
to her ribs as if
in walking that way
no matter how temporarily
it would lend itself some
how to memory
yet now it is already remembered
'If you insist' he had said
and allowed her to listen as he played piano.
The art of caring; that facility she felt in him.
Earlier he had listened to the heart of a sick man.
Observing his giant Blakean muscles.


What else is there
she thought
but the touching of others        however brief
tight between fear.

## Drought 1976

        To what can the heart be blamed
empty buses wind up hill and dry pavements
        where local dust has remained now
for weeks. Loud as unfettered as a lion
        I make my roar silent as bush fire
that creeps here in South London to take hold
        of kerbs and sidings until they
belong elsewhere. "I don't mean to abuse the
        water but it cools and cleanses and I
cannot resist." To what can the heart be blamed
        golfers strain their muscles in the heat
and arrogant schoolgirls hover in ones and twos.
        If the night were only the night
and darkness confined to dark shapes that are
        seen to be birds. Three quarters moon
the larger breath of all things. Blond beyond
        blue your eyes, we change and are as frail
and soft as a crayon.

"*Which is neither mine nor his but in common.*"
*for Barry*

And how much do you know
of being my main concern.
The sun at its zenith as the
'Orphanage of the Tender Tiger'
is with us for another year.
As if
it were only I that was meant to be
still, dark,
listening at time devour its
useless motions to what the personality blames
itself for; small to be afraid that tomorrow
we will not be seen in winter.
Ripen trees.
The lake at ice point.
A hares breath away we measure by.
Someone has placed a lost glove on the fence.

Morning teeters on the fine edge of sparse trees.
I intend to be early, bright and credulous as
'looking forward' is the key to eternity.
So tell me how much do you know of being my
main concern.
"It's not catastrophes, murders, death, diseases that
age and kill us; it's the way people look, laugh and
run up the steps of omnibuses."

Robins arrive in the bleak climate.
His red turn.
This,
love, for you, in winter,
brightly blue.

## This time of year

As when daffodils are on the turn for
bees to suck at pollen before rest, to what
can the heart be blamed.
Women trudge the High Street make Bank Holiday shopping
lists and children eye Chocolate eggs.
This warm open air on our necks as we loosen
a tangle in the hair or readjust a scarf.
In the street the backs of people as they
sniff and exhale and move off in cars and are
gone; sky changes are not observed.
The sun rose up again today as it does this
time of year. On the verge of leaning against
tears I watch the early tips of trees through
a square of glass. Take this life towards it,
outside there are rooftops and eaves,

## Distant Tender
*for my Father*

Your last sight of snow
brought the end to a life that gave that gave.
    Now the first white hairs on my mothers head
    come as I show snow
    to my daughters
    their tiny hands take hold and ask
    "What are we going to?"

Upon the earth
wind, sleet, snow, gale.
There is much coldness among the world
we learn to warm the fears of others
on our loss.

## "Tell them how easy love is"

How the light mist comes up and across
the marsh in late afternoon
how the big trees are so big.
If I was a man the love of a good woman
would keep me safe and wear me out.
Tiny flowers in the wood tonight
I picked a few and brought them home.
Crow and sheep share the same water trough
just the way the light rises
up drawing together the day and the voices
of the people warm in their homes.
O tell them how easy love is.

## Waking up in America
*Mass. U.S.A. 1975 for Fred Buck in whose house it was.*

"Is that Spider Man Daddy?"
asks Ketty, I turn over and ask
Barry to move over –     "For crying out loud"
he says. Outside sirens and machinery
bright sunlight and boats.

Boats in the harbour
Herring Gull shrill

Sore eyes. Salt wounds
men at midday.

Under the sky    rolling Lobster rock
and wail and loose their souls,
too easily for my liking.

Children learn by kindness
we touch their smaller limbs.
Yowling items in the kitchen, but
still they grow and turn and breathe
and ask nothing.

I am finding it easier to be casual
perhaps it is the way of my body
changing as it does
daily
casting off all kinds of ailments with ease
and mercy. Yes I find it easier to be lighter
soon I shall blow away without
any bother at all.

## Case Note

The first hot days of the year
girls move about the town in last years
summer clothes and the men with rolled
sleeves or bare-backed paint houses and thatch
moves in the villages.
I admit into hospital a woman who calls me
the devils advocate and Princess Anne, her
delusions hallucinate her dry.
Later an urgent phone call sends me to the
caravan site where Jim, out on bail, tells me
that if I don't give him money for his wife
and child he'll rob a bank. I tell him to rob one for
me too while he's there. On his arm is tattooed
'born to lose.'

## I prepare myself for the sight of myself

As in territory alone
        fear is encountered
and once looked at
        realised for the hollow air
that it is.
        That stance we have and see
in passers by
        like the face as it
contorts
        as it moves up the hill
in friends
        the sight of ourselves.

## Open Letter

My dear
I would be
as it were
caught into action of non action,
drawn as I am
to the pavements of this town
the low ploughed fields of Kent.
And missing you, as I do,
there is nothing
but space
and I walk into rooms
and study the plants again and span
the length of raw days with my palm
"and a sob comes
simply because its the coldest
thing we know."
So you leave
and the climate is holding
I long for silence
and thin air.
Often we are vague and small
at the end of a day.
Briefly encountered
who sees him as to
feel him
it is in dying,
apparent sunlight
so often we
prospect after dark.
Street lights grow old
ghosts on my sleeve.
Autumn could find me out,
running my hand along the cut edge of
Kentish flint.
The purr of your teeth

along my lip,
tender
it haunts
and I fall in.
Youth sketches the horizon
alone in cloud.
For so long now I have spoken
of touch without fertility.
I have used up the sepia of afternoon
my hands are numb.
Wounded water, it rains
teeth within anothers mouth.
Taut against circumstance
meet daily gall of human tears
that are ribbons of attempt.
Woodsorrel. The dream is tender.
Will you flash your fears at me.
Rubbing the hand brings blood to the surface.
"The trivial rain, it's sparkle on grass"
Laurel Nobilis
I would give you this
to mark the things you love.
Velvet Magnolia Tree.
It's that simple.
The things we admire in others we own in ourselves.
Of us all in our better moments.
Arms linked in sleep
anxious wakers that we are.
Rooks on the Marsh making their nests high
in the trees about the tiny grey churchyard.
My dear
the evening moves on. The swans flay themselves into the
telegraph wires.
Tight buds of Hawthorn
I am below surface again.

Bitten by it we conjure with touch.
My dear,
you are day worn at the end
of demands.
You fall asleep almost instantly
male tiredness it is of such.
Warm bones and young stubble.
Bells prompt
us of lives firm within this peculiar electricity
we call hope.
When stars cease to be light giving and take in all
that is around them they absorb without giving.
We must
"remain worthy of fire
like a poet growing older."
The Wagtails on the green at Wookey
a late afternoon
I have befriended myself yet again.
"She was looking for reasons to unlove him"
Air so solitary it could only be likened
to the Hepworths in the park. Her heart like
a Robins egg.
The years are getting shorter
certainly they press for some
fine line within me for
I have seen the evergreen replace itself
and the pink stones by the waters edge
but my dear I am drawn to the
chalk hills of Kent and the pink orchards
will find me knee deep in autumn leaf
alone.

## To see who you might be

Holding ourselves up to the light
      our lined palms.
The way one life crosses through another.
    All hope is investment.

"A lone quiet life
still she held it closely
as though it would cure her of any malady."

A whole season has shifted in on me
      tired Sparrows see us move off
These heady years!
A stray hair of yours on the pillow
my heart is the whalebone of me.
Skin and earth you track me down to
a patch of land which burns as I sleep
I astound myself by my misused strengths
solemn at my nakedness at all times.
Urgency utter urgency.

## I am touched by your fear

As we walk out from the coast
into these rural villages where
the women become bored and wait
for buses back into town.
I am troubled by the idea of moon
and how one year comes upon another
leaving me here with the cows who
never sleep but lean against the field
to rest.

You chance into sleep, the white limbs
of the young trees behind your head.

## On sighting the first bluebell
*for Chaucer*

My eye is my heart
I cannot go further
Bluebell
breaks
the sticky sap heals
at once a dream of waking
the Bell has its safe place
easily sliding between showy shoots
Blue present of early May
I smell the Blueness of it
quite returned

## Dusting

I sweep the floor and dust
the furniture.
O dust fill of earth, leaves,
branches, stones, chalk,
cardboard, tyres, rain.
Particles of bird, mouse,
flower, vole, bee, cat, tree,
chair, curtain, eyelash, postman
and moth.
O dust of shop, wellington, paw,
mouth and starling.
O dust carried in the air from the
fire, from a car, from a foot,
from plane, from lip, from speech,
from a bus, in coal, in wood, in paper.
O dust brought from miles away coming
here to rest in this kitchen only to be wiped up
moved on, taken back.

## Bitten by it we conjure by touch

A late bird across the
darkening sky sky
as if
it were
shaking me
these thistles so
fill of seed the air
disturbing
these ginger trees
high road above
valley, shadow
these alert me
youth and large
night
we are truly
young in the
centre of force
the courting couple touches upon
touching swooning
It is this fear
this total fear
of nothing           so
permanent
that leads me to this
ache for     your hair
it is seen   a handful of leaves
quick longing    autumn

And above on the
sky     high road
leading down
to the valley
where the courting couples
touch and swoon

is alive
with an urgency
that is
found in
folds of dew where
now it twists
even over what
seen as urgent
as a mans wrist
this which

others lives
so carefully
so

so
urgent

# This restlessness: this ache

Our chipped hearts!
Your forearm across my body: at night
the gift of one another
how it holds me to this temporary axis of living.
The luxury of breath
that brings the idea of you,
talking in bed, a movement of hair
falling across your neck
causing my life to shift with this
restlessness: this ache.
The divine family of light
Vivaldi's Winter Song.
38 hours of solid rain, how the unlikely warmer
air of summer haunts me. Here the cats
asleep on my desk, a rushing of air/high
hard wind along this coastal town where
off season waiters lean in doorways and old people
shudder to the Post Office.
Your head on the pillow, waking from sleep
before a working day
this restlessness: this ache.

## This, our frailty

Hands which follow clay
touch skin:
the heart young again.
Beige reeds on the river
    this wintered place.
A water rat moves across the river
we mark his course. A flurry of
migrating birds, the disarming of you.
The life of creatures and plants below
water. Seeing the hours of you move
    through my hands.
On a night wrought with storm, sealed by gale
– we exchange this our frailty, love.
Stealth, constancy, take the urgency from my
body for "I squandered the summer away without
love". Woodsmoke, warm flagstone beneath
the feet, a simple measure of our hearts' smallest
hope.

## Diary of a Working Man

His arm is a brace
of pigeons.
Shouting across the yard
the figure darts forward
slumps back, drops.

A bird tears his eye
Panic and night
his son was born on the
horse-hair settee – later
he mopped the floor with towels.

The instrument was obviously
Power
less all else.

Spat down the tunnel
with a scream of fluid on
his tongue.
Singing with such belonging
at the match.


Again the yellow madness.
Light cloud –
early shift
across the track.

Coal, sweat, oil, pay
thats how it was
falling out of the tight throb
at 11.15 and still two hours left.

Like turning a wet
shirt inside out
the room was inside his overall.

Bird song from a long way off
Exceptional death.

The sky has run out of ink and
awful hatred for her skin.
He goes out to the corner
past the ironmongers and the men
carrying trade plates.

Blackened aspic hell – shrill
light in the aviary above tears.
Even this is shown to be free from
an emblem of chance
up against the bar.

'Shrivel' the doctor said
'you are a cloudy apple' (spit at
anything but her and your pale son on
the ochre hospital seat), the horse hair
settee, later I..
Earlier light cloud across her neck as she
put out bread for garden birds.
Even here the flies die along with the rest
in the lampshade –
moth, cheese, apple, porch
fold toward nothing, toward the green curtain
he put up facing the street the night she died.

Ears in the machine.
Bite at this
come up with tar.

What's left
is the in
ability to eat alone
leave a room
completely bare.


The bird is well into the
centre of the wood.
Bright worn hands hold the parcel
and journal of song.


Throaty fire that would
burn even the sceptical skin
of his shoes.
A small perfect bolt alone
with spare change on the bus.


Not just ability
to position the eye
for vision/ but ability
of ear to despatch.


The sun has made a fire of his hair
a certain finality of nothing shames him.
He stands upright against the tree.


Creosote/air/lather
on his metallic smile
that night he walked to the station
and thought
are these spirits or fine Oaks.

The bright yellow beak startled
him into grief
The cold tap dripped all night
continued into midday –
wild with anticipation of new voices.

Some men stand around a car
on the edge of the motorway,
further on a girl crosses the street
in a nylon overall.
He cannot take his coat off but walks
into the university of the tree.
The pilot has caught his breath in a
distant vapour trail.

Man belongs to man.
Dry your eyes with plates
the moon is quite ready.


Between distance. Tears hum on
his evergreen collar    space of winter
trees, the ivy that gags his veined
ankle.
Sleep and almost sleep, the son
wakes, panic flickers on haunches
at the back door.
Wet    sharp    loom.


The last stop on the line.
Clock in with the war damage
brown rooms.
"Imperfection breathes creativity
grit produces the pearl. We are

responsible only to that filth
that we allow to sleep in our dimension.
Nobody is forever a stranger to another."
He walks across the floor.
Outside the wind is bleak with
human torment,
a blade of grass tickles the sky
bright blue.


He took her hand
the pale skin
fingernails formed accurately
hair shaft caught on lazy eyelash.
        O
to never be outside of this.
    "Come outside,
    the air is cool,
    possessed by love
    with no option."
He kissed her. The green light
of the pub car park behind them.


The afternoon
The sparrow bathing in mud.
He turned, would that she were
touched now restored with glimpse.
Night is a pale shadow to sleep under
his head dark on the pillow. Small.
Silent.
Break the fall with tears and dream.
Outside in the wood, primroses, two women
and a dog, the earth climbs right up
behind the pregnant trees.

## After USA

Coming home
all the buttercups are out
lambs adolescent shorn so they
look like young pigs.
It's so hard. It's so green.

What gift is there to buy a child
one who needs so little and wants so much.

I wonder what all this is about
maybe you've never thought of it before.
Perhaps I'll just go home and wait.
If only we could have love without paying for it.
But then there would be action
and the hair
falling across your neck
would be hair falling across
or hair falling
or neck
no hair
just movement somewhere.

## Something you can recognise
    *for Mike Booth*

Could it be
    the light coming in through the window
    just damp with condensation from the washing
or is it
    the field as seen through cupped forearms
    explaining the shape of the hill.
it may be
    the line of hair on a mans arm leaning
    bending slightly crooked.
or is it
    the hedge outside seen through tears
    and the little trees all clustered
    together and the river slipping by
    and the sky in pieces bright blocks of blue
    with cloud.

## Six Pieces From The Sauna

1.
Life without men is such a relief she said
their strong hands and hair curling across
warm shoulders. You can do without it she said.
All that dressing up and the looking and the
wait and the hope.
What a relief she said to be without hope.

2.
Luck.   I was born lucky – without it. She said
and laughed.
At the nurseries today a coachload of young bronze
Dutchmen came and looked round the tomato houses
and all the girls came out and flirted. A whole
coachload of men and who do I get
– the female teacher comes over and talks to me about
tomatoes.
Luck. Don't talk to me about luck.

3.
I told the judge I did when it came to court
I don't want no maintenance from him
he can keep his money
but you can't reason with men can you
and he made me take £4 a week for the girl
but of course he never paid and we had to go back
to court again and I told the judge then
– his money stinks worse than he does I shouted
and I don't want it and he don't want to give it.
You're a special sort of woman the judge said
and it made me feel all sort of glowing and happy just
to see an important man like that say those things to me.

4.
O the effort to be healthy she said
as she sweated away her huge limbs on the wooden slats.
Ten years I've worked on that Hoffmann press
for ten years that metal bar has stuck into my side
look – she said and showed me the dent in her leg where
the machine had established itself. That's why my legs
are so huge, she said. All that standing – you can't
stand for ten years and not expect a result can you. She said.


5.
They measure your legs and then they wrap you up in those bandages tight as you can stand and then they cover it in cold stuff like unset jelly and then they leave you. We didn't half laugh. Then they take it off and measure you again and let you hold the tape measure so's theres no cheating and its great. I lost three inches off my hips and two off my thighs. Don't know where it goes – they say it distributes it.


6.
He was conceived because I got an electric shock. I was plugging in the washing machine and I had wet hands and the next thing I knew I was on the floor on the other side of the room with my arm and hand all black and the nails gone and the arm jerking up and down. I was in a right state I can tell you. I rang Mum and we went to the hospital. I was in for two nights. Well I never took the pill those two nights did I and when I got home he was conceived. I didn't give it a thought.

    But he died at eighteen months old. Hole in the heart. I'm not being awful or anything but it was best seeing how the marriage was wrong. I took him to the hospital almost everyday at one time but he died. Bill left the next day and he didn't even come to the funeral. He used to smoke Players and the morning of the funeral he put a note through the door on the back of a Players packet saying "Can't come to the funeral. I'm working". Not even Dear Sandra or signed Bill – just that on the Players packet. I didn't cry about the little one dying for three months. I had Theresa to look alter and I was all alone and then one day I lost my purse and I phoned my neighbour and she came round and put her arms round me and said "never mind love, there's worse that can happen" and it was her putting her arms round me like that did it . . . Suddenly I let go and cried and cried. No one had actually touched me for such a long time you see. I never cry to my mum. I like her, don't get me wrong, but she can't accept it when I'm weak. I always have to be strong to her otherwise she'll say what she always says – "You should never have let Bill leave you, you have to work at marriage you know."

### "A soft weeping like rain drumming on dry soil"

I can't settle this.
I can't sleep.
I can't settle this I can't sleep.


What's all this about pricey pain
Griegs Holberg Suite
the sun coming in through the curtains just
for a second or
two then takes off again
as
light
and as airy
as the poet ought to be
as allusive and careless as the poem is.
Winter wheat no where near ready.
Walking up the road earlier
sidings full of withered fruit
shed by some lorry or other vehicle
and now new shoots growing right up between the old fruit.

# Ownership

Sweeping a veil across
your face or a flannel across the mouth
its all the same
gift of a few hours
in what would seem like total possession
or a glimpse of
anothers passion.
Can I give more than a promise?
Or do we holler at the exhaustible
in the dark light cold night
of motorway
and do we not all come home alone
to our own cold reception or return
our faith of human over human.
I would give it all up if only you
would ask me or tell me
but then for you to say
or him to ask
or her to receive or his to give
or him to suggest
or she to give in and walk towards him
to answer
to surrender or his to let go of
or his to break down over or hers to allow
or mine to admit.
I pace between succour and the chilling fright of the gift.

And so much is already ours only we shout for it
like lambs in calf
demanding what we have no need of
surplus
and the hours of labouring in the tight dawn where I cried
at being so at being so
and damned the sky for its light
and if only it had been his to give and mine to have asked for

and theirs to have noticed and hers to be fearful and
to have fought and mine to give
be proud of and yours to have loved and yours to have loved
so happy with and if only we'd have taken more care
of shown the way to
and is it that measured and who is measuring who is looking
and in the dark sheets of her knowing he would never
be hers only the hollering
and mine in the giving
will you look out
will you look out.

Come on
the house is empty
the arms are full but the legs are a
way out.
O take the urgency from my body
He took her hand
she took his number
they walked back again she was certain he was
watching insecure
they took turns at laughing
he demanded
he moved she followed he turned round
she looked at him he looked away she sat up
he sat up they looked down he asked her she
refused blindly saying 'its no good'
he came after her she wasn't there
he wondered about it and she cried
he had tried again but she had already found him
he was pleased she was cross
they walked off together. She stopped trying
she stopped crying.
He asked why she said she hadn't he knew she had.
They ran back quickly she'd changed her mind

he changed his face
he came back they were turning the wrong way
he was hurt
she was pleased he was damaged she didn't want to know
he asked her again she forgot who he was
he wondered too
they remained and she wanted him
he wanted her
she wanted to walk
he ran and he fell
she went to him and cried too
he was pleased he was old
she was very old
they were looking at the same place in the sky
he said come on the house is empty
the arms are full
but the legs
the legs are a way out.

## Collecting sheets

from the washing line
take a pull at them
not before
seeing the tiny
sparklets
of frozen moisture
along the top for maybe a couple of inches or so;
the Great North star up above.
It's vital to be as we are
making no extra demand
as if
there could be anything but the cloudless sky
up and above and the cluster of stars
the quarter moon.

## It's very often not who you are but whose you are
*for Lee*

Watching you
walk upstairs with your tiny daughter
you stop
halfway to kiss her
looking first at her face
before moving off.
    So the hidden agendas we have inherited
bring us back to how and where we are.
From the bridge the late workmen on shift walk back
across the tracks
and we comment on the rail-sidings fill of distanced
flowers and seeds, perhaps from Peashooters you say.
Later we speak of the adult fears and the childhood
resilience, the hearts of poets arid vital acts of love
and endurance.

# Hard To Place

I

His mother, a petrol pump attendant, was said by those who knew her to be far less than bright. She had not wanted the child but had wanted his father. She grew very fat with the pregnancy but told no one of the forthcoming child inside her. On the forecourt of the garage she went into labour while delivering three gallons of four star. They stifled her screams with the rag that wiped the dip stick and mopped her waters with the sponge that cleaned the windscreens.

Now eight years later he's a tiny child and the doctors write notes about his small head circumference and his stammer. He has moved eight times in the last three years, he is a difficult boy. The woman from the home writes on his review form that he often uses situations to his own advantage. His gait is odd, she comments, and he frequently limps to attract the attention of adults.

II

Late one January night when the whole house was sleeping the young mother put her careful plans into action and slipped away from her family and its life. The three tiny children remained asleep until 7am and their father until 9. It has long been agreed that the woman has returned to Ireland and all efforts to trace her through the newspapers, police and Salvation Army have now been terminated. When the children realised their mother had gone they tried to ring her on their toy telephones and sent her letters through the Mr Men post office. They cried themselves to sleep most nights and have been constantly greedy for food.

When their father realised his wife had gone he spent the family allowance at the bookies and told the welfare that something would have to be done. He signed them into care and jumped beneath the Northern Line on the way home. It is true to say that the children with their 6, 4 and 2 years are a handful and tend to be clingy. Only last week the eldest boy was found asking a policeman to please find his mummy.

## III

It had all been too much one way and another. The fact that her boyfriend had been taken away in a police car that morning, her final demand from the credit card company had been delivered, the flat reeked of the damp and the child was fretful. She collected together her purse, pushchair and raincoat and set off for the shopping precinct. Once inside she felt better but the child moaned for sweets and the piped music mixed with the lights and her lack of food made her become dizzy. Sitting down next to an elderly couple who were rearranging their shopping, she enquired whether they would keep an eye on the child while she found a toilet. Two hours later the couple continued with their attempt to extract information from the wailing child. Eventually the precinct security guard took the child away and a police woman was called. The sobbing of the infant drowned even the piped music.

Now, four years later, the little girl has a new family who worry about her insecurity and dreadful fear of open spaces.

## IV

After her brother had been killed by swallowing the bleach she came into care. Her mother had asked that she be taken away before she harmed her. The last she saw of her mother was never to be forgotten, she has no recollection of her father at all but it is believed he works on a fairground. She frequently has terrible nightmares that wake the whole home. The staff say she encourages boys to come into her room, she has absconded on two occasions when the fair has been in town.

Her mother is now in prison and she has written to her but has received no reply.

The staff at the home would like her to live in a family to be taught some discipline since everyone believes she is promiscuous and could be in moral danger. She is nine years old and calls her dolly 'Mummy'.

## VII

Late one January night when the whole house was sleeping the young mother put her careful plans into action and slipped away from her family and its life. The three tiny children remained asleep until 7.00 a.m. and their father until 9.00 a.m. It has long been agreed that the woman has returned to Ireland and all efforts to trace her through the newspapers, police and Salvation Army have now been terminated.

When the children realised their mother had gone they tried to ring her on their toy telephones and sent her letters through the Mr Men post office. They cried themselves to sleep most nights and became greedy for food constantly.

When their father realised his wife had gone he spent the family allowance at the bookies and told the welfare that something would have to be done. He signed them into care and jumped beneath the Northern line train on the way home. It is true to say that children with their 6, 4 and 2 years are a handful and tend to be clingy. Only last week the eldest boy was found asking a policeman to please find his mummy.

## X

"All I know about me Dad is that he murdered my little sister when she was eighteen months old and I was five. I know that he was from Glasgow and only had one eye. My Mum came to see me just after I came into the home but she was very ill and they took her to a hospital for diffy people where she still is. I think being in the home with all the other children was better than being with my parents. I miss my little sister though. I hope if you do find me a home it won't be with diffy people, I've had enough of them." She laughs and shakes her head of yellow and green streaked hair. At thirteen years old she possesses the body of a woman and the warmth and humour of a friend. "I don't remember much about him doing her in really, only that one moment she was laughing because she'd pulled his newspaper to bits and the next she wasn't."

XI

What she said when I asked why she hadn't seen the children was that she had meant to but hadn't, she had wanted to but then as it had been so long that she though it best to stay away. Then she cried a bit and I asked her if she wanted a tissue "I want my f...g kids" she said. I told her she needed to show the court that she was responsible now and could care for them properly, she looked out of the window. "Why don't you take someone else's kids away". Then she spat. As she walked away she turned back and shouted "anyway you can have them, see if I care," I watch her angry back walk through the heavy doors.

When she came back she said that it wasn't me she was angry with. She told me that she had been twelve years old when her mum left her, she had never seen her since and hadn't wanted to see her anyway. "I can't be it, I can't love them enough."

She walks away pressing digits on her mobile phone as she walks out of the building, I watch her as she passes the hoardings on the roadside advertising milk.

# Raising You At Night
### *for Phoebe*

Be strong
    be honest and be fair.
Make   judgements with difficulty
    and know when others do not.
At night your child's arms and legs
    curl back into foetal pose.
You, my first born who suckled at night
    our tired moon and early milkman
saw us tussling to ease your baby pain;
    the adult ones I cannot cure.
Be strong
    be honest and be fair
see how the new day rises upon us so well.

## The Snoad Hill Poems

*for Ian*

1.

O house, O sloping field, O Poplar trees whose tall arms salute.
Bleating
Bleating everything is looking.   The cows call
                                                        at night
                                                        for their calves
                                                        removed alter
                                                        weaning. Four
                                                        days later they
                                                        give up
                                                        throats sore.

I am at a loss to cleverly describe the lights
from the tiny train in the distance snaking its way
south from London across the Kent land.
"A necklette of tynie golden stones or
a worm of saffron slipping through a lanyard of light!'


2.

                Walking towards the village
                the moon as bright as a cats eye
                thin film of cloud across the empty
                autumn fields.
                I am wondering you see about this
                thing they call chance . . .

                How it was that you and I became this way
                we hadn't noticed the sun lifting the
                trees upward . . . so much power in the trunk.

                The way we've chosen to arrange ourselves.
                The tired manner of the chin of an
                old person standing watching

goes up and down
seen it all before worn out.
Why are we always moving about?


3.
She had the stance of a Snowdrop.
It concerned him that already the wind had
been exposed to her face and that her
lightly chapped skin made an embarrassed glance
appear on her face. Perhaps it was all the crying
that wet her face.
The womans countenance was bright and her
unusually welcoming mariner was renowned.
"It was always thus" she said to him late one
afternoon as he packed the car "always it
is the woman who waits and says little."
Glancing back as he drove away he caught her
eye in the rear view minor and was reminded
of the first day he had seen her.
The air had been warm during the night and the
next day he had set off to town to buy
an extractor fan. She had been standing across the
road talking to an older man, her hand
on his shoulder, her head in his hands.
He was struck then as now that she was as pale
and thin as a Snowdrop and that if she bent
any closer towards the earth she would simply
snap.


4.
And if my light should
sudden peter out
do not grieve
thinking
I had not time to
admire the upturned leaves.

Just today I brought home
Rose bay willow herb
Cow parsley and fern
Germander speedwell
and this mitre headed beauty
is bright yellow Kidney vetch.
What more can you hope for.


5.
Digging up weeds by the little hedge
the spade hits the store of Bethersden
marble that is the foundation here.
13th century clay threw up Palidisa Carnifera
composed almost totally of fresh water snail
fossilised.
Cut and polished    so striking
Cranbrook and Biddenden pavements show the
pock marked broken down snail shells.
Cut and polished    so striking are
the Cathedral and nave steps in Canterbury
and Rochester, the Great West tower of
Tenterden church.    In the buildings of
Woodchurch and Headcorn and Hythe the finest
examples are found, the best seen of its value.

Pale and dark brown and blue almost luminous tints
feel alive when touched.
Gentle water snails skate in the dykes.
"It bears a good polish and is very hard
and durable if dug up in its perpendicular
state but if horizontally found it peels off in flakes."

Ox drawn sledges dragged these great marble
slabs to surrounding villages and to the lodges
of the masons who worked it.

6.
Our hands crushed
bent back against one another
we turn for warmth and find only dampness rising
from our troubled palms as if
all Cyprus trees were in troubled prayer.
The tiny branches and new shut buds of our unborn child
lay alert listening to the dark damp womb.
Walking out along Sparrow Hatch lane the exquisite woodsmoke
no moon but the sharp light from the London train
coming home South.
An alarmed creature in the hedgerow, turns round, sees me
and takes off.


7.
Its this familiar black line from the tops
of the trees making their way up to the woods
from the edge of the field.
Near the small white bridge the cows move off
Late Harvesters come home after dark
tractor and trailer lights blazing as they pass.
Inside me
you my first born move with such force, pushing organs into
your own shape. Coming to us, as you do, with nothing. I too
have nothing but these arms to offer and this heart from which
you take    life,
this comfort for always yours.


8.
Waiting
all of us
the jersey cow and her smooth red body swollen
tight with calf. Long tongue sucking up grass,
conkers hang
some darker than others, always they seem too early.
Acorns tiny in their cups rattle in the air.
Ease. Grace. I am won over and quite ready.

9.
Temperament is related to physique.
Heavy showers on and off all day soaking
into the dry earth. The first rain in three weeks.
Turgid stems turn small flower faces skyward.
"Jesus wants me for a sunbeam" I know he does.
In Georges garden a white lily has opened
up and made me think of him a week
before he died saying
"I'm so confused, I'm so old, it doesn't seem
at all right me being like this."

10.
The jetty
just before Christmas
the whole bay out there and the little boats
in the frozen water.
How else can we sharpen our hearts on the first
bleat of morning from our small bed where we lay curled
together in sleep.
Your dark ginger curls on the pillow and the autumn
leaves under the car headlights
are at night the axis for all this living.

11.
The hedge breaks out in bud
giving it that bullion coated tinge
we associate with frost.
Sparrows chip along looking to make nests
and the sheep lay close by too heavy with lamb.
"Why can't we go for walk and come back pleased"
The blackbirds glazed black body on the garden
post waxed against rain the sparklets of water
he shakes off before he sings before he flies.

## Notes one two

I

The garden birds listen
                  small heads cocked
on one side    alert for the movement
of worms in the fresh dug soil.

In the street people worry    talk about
ending it all. Pull themselves into new days.

II

Spring is here and I push my thumb against it
holding it back for you.    Tell me
whether once a small bird standing
                  on grass plunges to your belly
sinking heart
with daily catastrophe.
Just to be a voice in the park
where lone golfers
and straggling packs of Brownies gather and are strewn
across the Kent grassland founded on chalk
and no one is disappointed by cloud.

*"And show myself and everyone as we are so striving after everything, so looking."*

All this new growth and luck and love
the fledging inside me flickers and
turns sometimes sleeping.

My heart banging inside its frame.
We walk to make the best of ourselves.
O.K. Owl so you've had your say
tonight twit twooing hooting while the
Lapwings plummet and dive.
Carry the air and lead us
soon I'll have heard all
your wise intentions.
Primrose you
startle me
so.

## Beyond All Other

Beyond all other
fear
that we will be unloved
lost faded in our lives without
the golden mark of youth on our cuff,
there is the knowing that always
we are part.

Beyond all other
hope
love is
being wide open to another, total
vulnerability. An exchange of selves.

Beyond all other
desire
there is the idea of eternity
we listen for its ghosts
finding habit, pattern.

Beyond all other
love
there is this extension of self
moving out against the inertia
that laziness we call work.
Moving out in the face of all fears
courage.
Moving out towards desire
value creates love.
Love then is a form of work
of courage.

"What massive stones. What magnificent buildings."

# Songs for the Sleepless

> *"The womb's an unwieldy baggage. Who can stagger uphill with such a noisy weight"*

O frantic surgeon
on the blister of us all
in our vain attempts to reshape
our survival driven frames.
The clatter     the frippery of womanhood
it is impossible to do without it.
Will this person be seen winding wool
          be seen putting coats on children
          be seen being seen
          be lost among the loud others.
All the wasted worried hours.
The person does return safely
eternity spits on our new shoes.
Drunken pitfalls.

> *"She is fearful that in case there will be no next time and the future suddenly cease."*

So many deaths in one month
endings bitten with shock.
The mist comes down despite any tragedy
                                    any plan.
Out of the corner of her eye the map alters
– a gradual growth of trees, cutting down of shrubs
  lick of tarmac across the heart.
"helpless animals and men have difficulty learning
that responses produce outcomes."

"*You were too busy being. And you are too busy now. You couldn't spare the time to note down a few facts: how the sun and silence poured into the big room with the yellow curtains; how everything was never ending and expendable.*"

Tomorrow I shall.
Tomorrow time will be used as soap, to be spread
cleansed with.
Crying spells.
Perhaps soon the day will be an agonising howl
as the Donkey in the next field screams out at all human suffering
and ceaseless need.
I have almost given up hope of using the moment for that
    which it is
to take in sensually the second the open heart the open heart.

> "But the body, the body, the perishable instrument through which all work and visions have to trickle."

My futile legs!
They won't take me out this door across the lawn and up into that field and down the other side again!
Women sweat as their special pelvic bones grind apart during childbirth as endlessly hands are wet from wiping down tables, children, men, their own bodies. Keep crevices clean that no one will see, yell secrets to one another to improve bonding. Bonding/sweat is the common result of vision.
Ache body swoon O sweetness laughter.

*"The greed of plants doesn't seem at all disgusting."*

Male interest in food is also understandable.
A shift in the skyline.
Holding my Mothers hand that contact between inner and outer.
A sharp pain across the body.
Is rain simply water.
The history of human endeavour
Men hover on bridges quite abashed with wonder at the reproductive process.

*"Once you start speaking, of course, the agony lessens."*

Helplessness
Helplessness against what appears to be fate
Yours to swallow up
is instantly lit
into the way of the world.
Is my voice really so shrill
are all these actions so meaningless
in the face of tragedy everything
is wiped dry and put away.

*"All you can learn is ecstatic surrender."*

Reassure me that dark will follow light
that sleep will rock us back into wakefulness
the anger in your heart will turn to something
for the moth banging fruitlessly at the pane.
O level my fears into something useful
mould my tears into a harmless gesture
for the end isn't really the end only getting to
know our love better.

> *"Nothing is known. It is merely a comfortable deadening to think anything's familiar; it is an expedient blotting out of an inherited estate that's far too big for you."*

Even the walk through your arms is new
although the anticipation of it led me to feel that
I would have remembered it after so much hoping.
Bright red Rosehips across the river walk
as we discuss how many shades of green or is it brown.
I shall sew my heart with these webbed cob dewy autumn
ideas. The revelation of a new town is like the seduction
of a strange man.
Walk out     walk back     no one pair of hands
entices me so as the quick earth with its easily forgiving
deaths.

"Anything noted while alive? Anything felt, seen, heard, done?. You are here. You're having your turn. Isn't there something you know and no body else does. What if nobody listens? Is it all to be wasted? All blasted? What about pricey pain."

I wish I could say.
I wish I could say something about the way you looked
that day. I wish I could say something of the lamb as
it came out with your hand into the world and your face
your face.
But perhaps the silence is enough to remind us of the smack
of nothing and how tortured we are and so afraid for ourselves
and how empathy and love is our only tool.
Thin twigs of Beech chance the heart into a hope of
fresh mistakes
O caution and anger could breathe great fools of us all.

> *"They tell me that the endless repetitions of life and death are soothing, rhyming lullabys, patterns in the jibbering void."*

Heart beat.
A growing up and a bearing down.
Shall we rid ourselves of the same muddy pitfalls
in relationshipwrecks.
The day comes up and we all go down again upon ourselves
with an ear to the soil and a hand on someones arm.
Love is a repetitious dancer whose terms swoon us into
impossible demands and expectations.
The minors clever blood.
O female cycle patience blame allocation.

"Well keep your eye on the object then. And keep your hand moving."

Accept no replica.
Go after that idea of yourself.
Most plans get torn up or rearranged and passed on in one shape or another; generation to victim.

The window
the outside
It's air and rain
air and rain
'there are some things beneath and too
powerful than grief'
The clear vase of Nasturtium leaves.
Look at the others in such agony as they walk along the street.

*"Maker accept no rest. Listen tonight. Above the autumnal winds there's that possibility so wild with hope battering at the shrugging shoulder and the pooh poohing diffidence."*

So was that love no more full of intent than
to pass it by with a turning down of the palms,
a turning over of bodies and new leaves.
Brave men read other peoples letters.
We always do it. We always seek out with feet like
limpets at any encouragement.
Give yourself leisure and stop wandering around; give yourself
some good things.


The families go on and on shopping, piling groceries into bags and
bags into cars and cars into garages and garages
into driveways and driveways into plots that are alongside
of other plots and other driveways and other bags
but don't let that depress you.
It is such a fright to remain within anyone for very long.


We were together when we saw the little lights of the
town below us
come out of the darkness and shake us hollow with the
alarm of others lives.

> "Everything you are this minute flows away faster than a breeze. It takes pain to burn through time, to turn a spot on the wall into the centre of the world now and hereafter."

But then there is all that attempt
all the effort of non doing
all the sitting around and hallo
and see you
but then the Moorhens gather together each morning whatever
and the frosting trees are gladder than ever.
A pianist breaks his hands on the chords
but its only a temporary arrangement
like death it comes and it goes.
It goes away and without realising it
we are back again with our lips in shreds
with nothing to say but that its gone and we're alone
with the weather and the remarks of the trees
are but efforts to make the
trembling slower.

> *"What is it? Glimpses, flashes in the medley sudden revelations impossible to recall, except for their absoluteness – the rock revealed by lightning."*

Nothing shameful or spent.
Composers and painters are
poets are
shot to pieces
at the cool tablet of reflection.
Male tiredness is of such,
the bark of young trees
gentle objects roused by their dream of leaves.

*"The cheap Sparrows peck about in the dust."*

What else is there to do
but to go after a special index of passion.
Praise the long limbs of young men
and the downy hair on their brown forearms
and the edges of fresh white shirts
covering the sides of strong capable chests.
Knowing becomes loving.
It's not who you are but whose you are.
Local means safe means close.
On the motorway sparrowhawks loom over litter
bins and foreign trucks pass on the inside lane.

I can't settle this
I can't sleep.

> *"Everything would delight because it would have no connotations, no history, no meaning but its looks"*

I was waiting for someone to overwhelm me
but the light went on being
the light.
We have come to the end of this then.
A strong storm
water everywhere
bleaching it out
bleaching it out.
No one comes.
Shaping ourselves
cutting on clay on unions   bonding
learning what we bargained for.
All these couples making do with one another
tearing up their hope with loathing.

"*Owls are about. A cat complains. Children murmur with bad dreams. The walnut tree sways in a burdened way. The cats tracks wander suggestively off into the horizon. The pigs bang about in their pens.*"

So much contact in a day. Ways of making the shaking bearable.
We will never know the way we think of one another.
Neither all that goes in between the talking and the seeing:
it all goes by with one great yawn and a little sleep,
we recoup over night and time does it
sparrows do it
the wet grass of the field does it
the light in the sky manages it.
All spent all spent all given up to the
misty evening
all this and the evening light
no one else nothing.

> "But I could have told you it would be like this. You should have said to death 'o death, it is better to keep you in mind remembering every moment how short time is, and what a concentration is necessary to get you where you're going or where you hope to go."

To look and find that the palm of your long white
fingers and hair curling was only the light from
the car headlamps as you turned the other way and the
fear of falling is
the idea of waking is
the ideals of hope are
only the light from the houses
soft trees as if warm liquid were
the line of a mans lip
the idiot heart
china heart.
What it all seems to amount to is a ceaseless agony to know
that all is well,
forgiven accepted and known
full face on. The rest is a grid of controllable text.
I was with you when you said that I had presupposed on our love.
I shook the tree and nothing came but the wind falling through
arms O empty arms.
All these agonies making do with grief.
It passes
yes goes so fast and the place where you stand can only be your
own. I have no idea whats coming next – I can only hazard at the
movement in the trees.

*"Women with gusty voices pound pianos in pubs. Impossibly happy against great odds. More ravaged and more successful by far than you, they know how to back-slap life with a greeting of gratitude."*

Across the fields here I lose my heart
where the mushrooms come up in seconds
with the damp and the sun and the watching out for.
Hunger for another
is part of this growing into
after that its just a falling into patterns
but until then I suggest that women walk alone into
the arms of one another.
I wish all this would go away
all this watching and waiting for no reason.

> "Other people must know more, I think. Who? Who is whirling on in virtuosity and can throw a brilliant sudden torch into this obscure bog where I don't even jog on."

None of them appear to clatter on and on
they all seem so damned happy.
If the nights get any darker I shall need
more than the sun to get me up.
Do I tell people about myself or do I
let them find out? What is essentially required
– is it already on my face? Can this be that easy?
Almost everyone has met someone else.
Is it only the newborn who aren't alone, is it the
cutting of the cord that sets off all this separation.
Is this the information that the others have.
Is that why they look.

> "Can love keep us from need? Needs are bolting in my garden, lanky and green irresponsible with unsuitable conditions."

Who's to say where we go and where we've been.
We go knocking on the wombs heavy door and out again
into the waiting kerb of sweltering knowledge.
Others have been here sick with ideas and no feet.
Love saves us from ourselves, spins its
chaotic fuse into our mouths.
Outside the cows never lift their heads intent on their
function.
Its so humiliating to be caught so with all this
gaping envy hanging between our legs for no reason.

> *"Those to whom the day is a weight to be borne and dropped for relief at night. Those who come nosing into the evening like dogs kept back too long."*

On the boxed estate the pubs
are billions with the street.
Under stone pavement slabs drains
and sewers pulse about with black
casualties.
In the morning the first paperboy clanks a gate
stirs a woman lying face down in her bed already
awake and watching his shadow move across the
room as he dresses to leave.
Why wait for it to
happen
go out and dig at the
suckers in the garden.
Your body – its angle
just keeps me hanging on
waiting for you.

> "This endless exterior is your remedy. Wrinkle out every
> ounce of life. That is the work in hand. It's a sweaty
> excavation"

Experience is a clammy joy.
We stood in the garden that night
and heard the childrens voices singing
in the dark two miles away at the Guide
Camp.
A few days later we drove past them
as they stood between the fields and the
edge of the road.

The Nightingales       The Nightingales       it seems
have somehow left off singing to us these last few
nights and instead       I'm finding the small dead
frames of tiny bats and the larger soft bodies of
moles.

I wish the Seagulls would stop hammering this
sense of loss into the memory of that first day
we came to this town – the damp and your sad lungs.
My running from it and the ache the ache
the impossible sick ache of it all.

> *"But here you must go to your office looking sprightly with a sparkle even if synthetic in your eyes. For who dares to stand up and say, We are weary O christ but we are weary."*

Of all things and their celebration.
In the photograph my Fathers long
boned hands hold my entire frame as
a new born baby. His face is that of
an angel.
But you must go out on the course again.
Keep loading the shots
for to be in danger is to look
and not wait but pass back across
the waste where the sleepless lay waiting.

## If You Have To Push It May Not Fit

My hands
have changed recently
the skin is rather papery
crinkled foil like
the veins stand out
like small rivers.

Let's face it.
They have been over doing it lately.
Never at rest
always putting on
fastening
pressing down, into, onto up to.
Smoothing out,
cleaning round
pushing back, applying this and that.
Making effort.

The light is blinding
I have over stretched my body
and now it has told me so.
The spirit too willing but pain
dampens its ardour.
The easy tears blotted now by the Daffodils
and Wood Anemone.

The children's arms are like tiny stems
they injure me with such fresh sap.
My soft lips are tethered
homeless.
The muffled world presses its giant mouth
onto my chest.
I must wait my turn
the blackness boasts a terrible hunger.

# We Must Learn Not To Breathe
### *In praise, Paul Auster*

The high rise flats; our openness.
Long marshland and seascape
quick growing Kale the
many stones.

Pylons. The lead air.
We have turned to phlegm.
The moon     is as quiet as an owl.

We have broken our promises
made alliance with the rain.
This is where the heart is
inhaling the dark.

'To live in this air we must
learn not to breathe.'

The children on the estate clamour
for attention, urgently draw for me
wanting pen and paper, adult attention.

We have rested
together
leant against those huge stories. They tell me
it is for the heart to suggest problems
and for the intellect to solve them
just for the time being.

# Kent

Our mute hands.
December rises over the tops of the trees
 can we miss so much with our arms
 high above the night. Consider this:

 The railway threading its polite
 thud lulling cattle deep in Barley.

 Our home lit up with love nestling
 into the ink black night. Swallows
 and Starlings. Pheasants and Owls.

 All chance germination snapped into
 bones, stems, trunks, feather.

A ribbon of sky. I want to talk to you. There are
so many things.

Black square. White edging. Dice. Clip your quick eye.
Ringed ferment clatters
The snow has made a primrose of itself.
Make a note if you can:

 The elderly neighbour walks each day
 further and further from his home
 soon he may not return.

 We play one another off against
 the other and yet there are no winners.

 The stench of mortality shuffling through
 all these mad-made things. Banter. Electricity.

A thin stream of water. I am hoping to cross the bridge
before nightfall. Cool the ice.

Frozen river and bleak roadsigns tell me that your heart
is at the cleaners.

# This belonging, this us
### for Ian and for Phoebe and Beatrice.

*"Only love gives parents any, authority. Parents who love each other can build something that the children haven't had time to build, and the children can see that and respect it. But when love fades and wears away into nothing the parents are like two petulant children, as petulant and unreasonable without the high spirits of children."* — J.W.

Our tiny childrens hearts are lanterns
of promise       we are led
and in turn lead by the moss stones      the coral
bark of stripped chestnut wood.
Forgive my hands
        their shakeness. The rivers
dark silt tenders less. Take hold this steady heart.
Forgive my tears
        their wetness. The crumpled
papers damp hand. Remind me of the short seasons
that can cut off a young life.
Forgive my greed
        its youthfulness. The dark trees
at night are only the dark trees of the daytime.
Give up worry and torture.

Life is O.K.
It has a lot to recommend it.
By and large.

He lifted up his head.
He lifted up his head all branched made.

Women snap
break the tender days
trapped between their bowed bodies
                guilty hearts.
Childrens small fears, open faces
trusted and held. Taunt the womens thirst of love.

Gladly gladly suckle.

## "Men Must Live And Create.
### Live To The Point Of Tears." (Camus)

*for Polly Hartcup*

I have been touched by the lives of others
brought home
to their beds by the sullen silence
of their wrists.
Experience is a comb
which nature gives us when we are old.

The worn warm ways of the world
weary with repetition
it is the only form of permanence
that we see.
Our learning
does not come from only our sorrows
look how common is our blood.

## "Who Takes the Child By the Hand
##                Takes the Mother By the Heart"

Scabious   paper white
turn inside out making the
everlasting eternal gift one heart inside another
like carrying a baby inside of you
she said
my heart forever with yours like that
as a mother is
knowing where the worry is.
My neighbour here died suddenly
planting willow planting oak
the hurricane killed him
she said
never recovered from the shock
of seeing the devastation
couldn't think where to start
so he planted
just planted too many.
As his wife
knew
some things as a wife
you just know
his heart in mine
like that just petered out.

## The Path Between the Yew Trees
### With Grass and Damp With Dew

I
"The simplest lessons are those which are taught last."

Often by those we least consider.
Humour.
The sun goes down on our minor
squalls and makes rainbows of our fears.
Illness.
Rest. The sleeping willow does not
ask for water waits for rain.
You won't be as you are now again.


II
"For the first time I have noticed
the lost and the lonely, how, with their
curious apologetic gait, they move through
the world like strangers."

Others stride with determined hatred
some amble honest and humble to salute.
Apology. Accepting triumph
welcoming sleep
watching the dark green trees, the pale
green lawns.
Sitting.
We are sinking beneath the soft stones
of the wearisome. The blue the blue
Anchusa, Delphinium, Purple eyes, green
skirted Viola.

III
"I hoped, I think, that she would recognise
in me what I had already discovered in myself."

It is perhaps that understanding which shakes
the tall cyrus tree, calls the infant to sleep.
Pretend the sky is only a mouthpiece, the
rain shifting in on the earth.
Lemon trees
    fireflies
the handles of the, drawers are shaped like snails.
A lane with high          overgrown hedges.

Seeing through the trees    to the water in
                                  the pasture. The
                                  Wren sheltering the
                                  tiny nest.
Loved and worried for
the children lay asleep adored, cherished, tired
with sun, with the demands of adults.
We sleep under the bright blue painted ceiling of
golden Nightingales, sun and moon.
The crickets and frogs sing together
patiently safe in the pocket of the valley.

The quotations are taken with thanks from Peter Ackroyd's book,
*The Last Testament of Oscar Wilde.*

## The Shape Of Things
*for Frances Presley*

Having long come to know him and
respect and worry
for the things she saw that mattered
her eyes turned away at the idea
of him
      with another.
The spring in his curl and the way one leg
crossed gamely
      before the other
she vowed never to sleep willingly again
she would
instead be lost in slumber
not asleep
merely dreaming.
Grant O Lord
she said
any careful plans for nakedness
      for rest
My heart has long been
in formalin
stained puce white.

# It's Easier Now

1

What is left of my Father's harvest
has lapped into the soil to bear fruit.
The birds have that look about them
I saw them thirst and suckle.
Tethered against the moss stones the tiny
violets shy away from fame.
Without the energy to form a shadow he moves
through us into laughter. The light breeze
against my foot, minute ideas chase the tip
of the afternoon. Nightingale heart.

2

Dream air. Flap away you quiet hours.
The heart is but a token of the body.
Stubbled visions and the hair runs wild
with blazing ink.
Walking like this O floss O talcum:
A bright stream of sunlight lights up your hair
but I can't say how this holds me here. Hold on
to that piece of your target. The dry weather
has made the nettles lose their sting.

3

What are the poets doing tonight?
Rounded mouths fill with petals
my arm is lost. It's only paper
on which they write. Despair
maroons. Walk on glass. Sleep on stilts
and eat water.
In the dust skulls wake up.
Look we don't love like the flowers
we haven't got it in us to be that
open.
Of exit and idea it's a wanton
access across your shoulders.

4

I try hard.
The geese in the moonlight. A bloated stiff
dead chicken drowned in sheep dip, white daisies
under my lips my gums have cracked with effort.
All swimmers must take the plunge. It's too easy
to be still let me light up the mud.
My face is lined. A map in retrospect.
Revisions response issues we see we feel we read
we turn over a new leaf and
find no index.

## Run Down

In the dark by the Reservoir the lights
        move
            flash on and off.
    My heart is irregular temperate like the
weather; I hear its dangers. I plant the
bulbs slowly this year.

Out in the fields even at dark the men
feed animals shake down hay, level the water.
It is a world we have saved for.

Plums and zinnias in the market place
Old men buy seeds; their hands are like glass,
they touch their caps to me: I am not so old.

Time runs out on us, the person so quickly
vanishes there can be no preparation for the
final disappearance.
I miss my father
my daughters cannot hear his stories.

The strong bindweed in the garden
tiny lilac faces of the michaelmas daisy
upturned hopeful.
The children lay asleep dreaming of
pleasing me
sometimes I am not shouting.

## The Garden

Ripe edges sway into crisp
      understanding of winter
and its small deaths.
      Such solemn grace of things
asleep. Promises gone wrong
      Seeds sweat bulge into spring
and into a blue summer anchusa,
      delphinium, borage, poppy.
Blackbirds' opera of light
      are birds fearful of the future?
They spread and dart
      we watch and sigh.

*June 1990*

## After the Hurricane

Walking out to shut the chickens up
stars stell worlds
no moon;
so bright
so many.
The chickens shuffle
mutter at my visit huddle back.
In the house the children sleep
by candle light
electricity cables blown clean away.
They are dense solidly asleep —
is no one as tired as me?
The oil lamps blaze
a strange car passes.
It would seem that
children dance to resolve the world.
We tired old ones
collapse on the sides
prepare ourselves for death,
too much knowledge leaves little room
and time for experience.
I will wave my flag and retire.


(1987)

## Not What You'd Call a Religious Man

"They gave me the mattress job plenty of times. You know what that is, do you? They get two mattresses, one either side of you so you're sandwiched in between them. A raw meat sandwich. Then the coppers beat hell out of you. It bloody hurts I can tell you but it doesn't leave any marks. Ask anyone that's been inside, they'll tell you." I ask about his family. "Oh my Dad's a looney, brain damage. I tried to murder him when I was 15 years old by beating him over the head with a cricket bat. He was very ill. I got Borstal and then the hospital wing when they couldn't contain me." "Did that help?" I ask with some degree of interest. "No way." "What would have helped then?" "Oh, I don't know really — maybe different parents, maybe not being one of 8 boys and having to fight for everything all the time. I tell you what wouldn't have helped for sure." "What's that?" I ask making careful notes. "All that religious stuff, that gives me the willies. Mind you I always got to church when I'm inside, not that I'm a religious man you understand, but you can do some good deals in the pews for a few smokes. Always worth a few blows the hymns are."

# I Said Hold Tight

I travel across the thick fog of the fens to the high walls of the male prison. After a long wait in the visitors hall where a prisoner is mopping the large floor in an angular, defeated way and the man in charge of the cafeteria has whistled three rounds of Rule Britannia and Silent Night, the man I have come to see arrives. He tells me he was several blocks away and there had been no one to bring him over, says he was playing his guitar, that once he played with the Rolling Stones before he was married, before any of "this lark" was his problem. He says there's a real big shot cocaine dealer on his wing — Director of a very large public company — headman, the police don't want much publicity as it might "do damage".

We talk about why I've come —he says, "Well Sherry's not my kid, you know — not mine at all. I thought she was, I saw her being born and I was pleased to have a little girl. Then one day I came home after work and see her sitting on a man's knee, I said hello mate who are you, he said I'm her Daddy — I said hold tight I can't hear that."

"Then I left and never saw the other kids until last year. Well, if you're worrying about how I could cope with them I'll tell you straight, none of them will end up in here. I've just been moved from that Army run prison, it was great, cleaned by squaddies, run by officers — they was wary about us at first, then they got interested in talking, especially when they found out that most of us had been in the army at one time or another. Yeah, they talked. I like talking."

"I've never had a driving licence but I've *been driving* since I was 9 years old. My Dad taught me — he was a costermonger. I got my licence taken away before I ever got it and now I'm banned till 1991 — I love cars. It's all I know."

"I know the offences my son's done are wrong and he'll know that by the time I've finished with him. I know he worships me but hold tight — he wants to be a policeman you know. Well can't say as I blame him — you meet a lot of interesting people.

I tell him that the court's unlikely to allow him to care for his son when he comes out of prison.

"Hold tight lady," he says, "I've got a three bedroomed house when I come out of here — and I'm starting a taxi business — all legit. It will be so legit even the big shot cocaine dealer what's in here will be a fare."

## (Untitled)

In the dark by the Reservoir the lights
        move
           flash on and off.
        My heart is irregular temperate like the
        weather; I hear its dangers. I plant the
        bulbs slowly this year.

Out in the fields even at dark the men
feed animals shake down hay, level the water.
It is a world apart one we have save for.

Plums and zinnias in the market place
Old men buy seeds; their hands are like glass,
they touch their caps to me: I am not so old.

Time runs out on us the person so quickly
vanishes there can be no preparation for
a final disappearance.
I miss my father
my daughters cannot hear his stories
will never know his games.

The strong bindweed in the garden
tiny lilac faces of the michaelmas daisy
upturned hopeful.
The children lay asleep dreaming of
pleasing me
sometimes I am not shouting.

*September 1990*

# In Revenge of Civil Disorder

*"There is much coldness among men because we
dare not to be as cordial as we really are"*

I

Mottle abuse.
Begin and crown the child
with anything but this;
A false ardour of final steam
its powerless intrusion.
Molotov during field study
measures blunt growth with
the axis that reluctantly
swigs at an excessive tear.

II

Retailiate against the foetus
with heavy discontent.
Street archers move off
suddenly into dusk – their reversed
parables; Love in a bitter disease
of mock care.
We are trespassers in our own clothes.

III

No heather there
not soaring to be done
between dances – hyper
nothing.
My embrace is wet from walking
in the river
– shoes run off swearing never
to smile again.

IV

Frantic collision into last week's
observation – you
th and the heath air – It's so close
it cannot be seen.
My clothes are saturated.
I am not worthy of forgery
nor am I the first to arrive.
Better sink with fire
headway up stiffle with rem
ember
ance and arrive here to answer
that confidence is not knowledge.


V

Search my flowered mouth
– but disarm, turn to run between it –
final and sweet,
Or,
immunity would bleed us
hollow as concrete.
We would be thin enough to leave
without being noticed.

## Against the Air

The bright edge of the woodpecker steals
Across the gaunt
Limb of sky
    We are already gripped as she
    Steadies
    Leans and steers into the mossed
    Centre of what is contained, known.

A dark feathering in the undergrowth of woodland
Our tired burdens draw into us
We tread without thought
    Driven by the flustered hope
    Again we are still unprepared
    And yet not asleep
    Or rested, even now.

The Northern stars are seen in the South too
Our poems are but small messages of quiet silence
Plain, empty, the air is against us as we try to make sense
    Evidenced by love of
    One to another
    We complete the work in our stride.

*November 1999*

## Along the Landings

Along the landings
shrill steam open vents to bathrooms
toilet seats lay open
fox holes
the bitter curve of the road where the toddler lay.
Rubbish chute
lit up at night the noise travels upwards
a belly button pierced
groans in the bedroom          his hand across her face
screams the glass into the vein.



Along the landings
lift shaft urine soaked cigarette stubs
"I'll get you for this"
torched front doorway boarded menace
the empty siren
lost from the flock the lamb waits while the others suckle
"I'll get you for this"
Washing hangs like a millstone
her neck
he saw her first          blue tattoo
nothing more.

Along the landings
the polished brass door furniture
keep themselves nice
the girl has plaits down her back and across the leather sofa
the money lenders gather about lights in their cars as they
    make notes, spin, take off.
There are buzzards about lining the trees before making a descent
Graffiti across the new door "wankers"
she sees it as she turns the corner
walks off again not even seeing
give me strength    give me strength,



Along the landings
brake dancing body moves fast
skateboard a sleek pencil movement
the rest couldn't catch him    too fast
Cars rev and line the alley they look out
Steady    a gaze lingers too long
"what you looking at wise boy?"
running he can do it
ducks down    rests while they miss him
Trees break out in bud before you know it the blossom unfurls
palm upwards.

Along the landings
the stairways concrete litter lottery tickets beer mats his
telephone number
part of it all.
no credit on her phone
he never did call
her face against his
over in a flash
her heart pounding worried late
worried late
worried
her mother knew recognised the look
washed her clothes            never said
tucked her in as usual "see you in the morning"
the pond lays open like a wound where the river meets it halfway
            seagulls cluster and then are gone.



Along the landings
the old lay still sick of it
waiting they listen it is shouting and it bangs about the menace
the upset and upheaval of it all        too late now
too late then.
The white cyclamen blooms all year the warden said so you
            can't beat central heating
the legs were once willing
it hurts
to leave
the chair
"I don't know" the nurse had answered when he questioned her
she had no idea
            no idea at all by the morning he would be gone
made sure of it.
The birds start up at 5 a.m. their brightness startles so.

All along the landings
the others have a better lot    benefits thriving visitors go come
"leave off" she said
"I don't want your fancy words its not what I need"
Refugee status    fledgling starling falls out of tree lays squeaking
the mother flies    willing it for hours    no bueno no go
pristine clothing aimless drifts loose less use
                                        less watching finding out
seeming solemn carrier bags.
"We can do without you" she said as it slithered from between
          her legs
"get you gone you" she said as it was cut and pulsed upon her.
They took her and the infant at her word    never again would he
          have that link
that blood that pulse memory that long that knowledge
that much.



Along the landings
a maze of promises and broken debris fades in
between the babies yelling
adult needs we need adult time we need we need time away
and soon enough they too are children    bleached ideals
white branches silver birched.
willing it different
"my Dad likes drills
and bimbos and doing
his own thing
he would come
only
he's    busy stressed out just now."
Magnetic keylock. Tradesman buzzer press buzzer and wait
          for entrance
she imagined him there waiting for entrance to the flat
the buzzer system dud but instead it was him

dud.

All along the landings
he threw up he threw the Hamster at the wall because
he said it shat on him
she ran out down the slope passed the bins the stolen pallets
she wouldn't go back and the Shoesave carrier bag was all she had
leave me out of this said her gran and she ran.

Beaten.




Along the landings
He was all that she wanted
warm
wanting her to be her
for that day
in April the trees were in bud there are so many of them
          bursting out new
like that
it was hard to chose
Tragic
nothing else to say his car left the road
no one else to blame
nothing.

Along the landings
They shave          too young.
Brazilian.          she wanted to be ready for him.
Instead
being cut
Wide Open
blistered with disappointment
out.
No messing
But it's done on the street in moonlight outside
The Club
Kissing and Kicking where it hurts
a lesson
learnt.
Keeping things tight
within the family.
It's a blessing
in sharp and deep disguise
Often
too often she would walk to the Offie for him
buy him booze
keep him sweet.
Returning the empty cider bottles
paid for the little one's crisps.

Along the landings
Welcome warmth
she tried to make a home
stair carpet with vomit where he staggered.
"When Daddy shouts my ears want to run away"
she lifted him up
pressing his heart against hers
"he don't mean it"
"he does, he said he'd kill you, punch your lights out. I love
             your light mum".
She looked away
Buckled him up
Dropped him
School Reception asked why he was late
dentist she muttered
"Mum" he said                X
she walked away.




Along the landings
Paint peels
revealing the broken dancers
half moon chancers, vodka chasers.
He caught he eye as she stood up
Saw her plastic see through bra strap topping
Her backless green dress.
The verges strewn with weed and thistle the hedges uncut
Broken down not like it was
Anymore.
Torn through the ripped up message

Along the landings
The price tags fluttered          strewn landscape on the
horizon of the tattooed knuckled stranger
who half jesting
leans over and asks for money as he
held a knife
to his throat a little too close
slipping as he did
and stamped on his feet
although and especially as he saw they were blistered swollen
            veins collapsed.
In her back pocket creased
the visitors permit to see him on the lifers wing
Terminal Alley he calls it.



Along the landings it has been a long morning
"My client would like you to be assured your honour that . . ."
the voice tails off as he looks over at her
she looks away
it was not
forever
like this
Once they
made
A child
together
Just them
One room
A bed
A moment                              ✗
the child
that now
they divide
tear up            throw away

Set apart.

along the landings
She reads
That the tsunami tragedy claimed a forty percent higher death rate of women than men. "A common thread runs through the different regions that explains this. Women were at home on that Sunday morning while the men were either out in their boats at sea, and therefore escaped the waves or were away from the shore doing other chores. Women stayed behind to help the children and the elderly when the waves struck. In Tamil Nadu women were waiting on the shore for the fishing boats to return so they could sell the catch when it arrived. Stories by survivors bring out another common factor Women did not have the strength to hold onto a child and also hang on to a tree or something else to save themselves from being battered to death. They could not clamber up trees with the ease the men could. In all these places, it was evident that women lost precious minutes as they tried to gather all their children before attempting to escape the cascading waters."
Precious minutes taken   lost
What could be more vital  than saving your child.
The beginning of it all.
he was never away from her
always in mind
his small hand in hers always like that she never let it go
she hoped that he knew it
some things she only knew
as a mother.


As he saw the wave he ran leaping across nets the wooden railing the siding stones
Others were screaming he saw them being dragged under and out and back in again.
Beyond his the trees on the edge of the village were too far, his feet bled but he scrambled up the tree his feet holding the edges as he had know been shown what to do.

All along the landings the lights go out
he cannot find the key to his home.
Still he
hammered
Empty silent the place did not move.
His mother was dead
She would not be at home for him again.


All along the landings the word is out.
At seventeen the height of creativity burning
mapping the skull
Bursting
unsullied
to
start over
stomach
recognize
re new.
cherish the spark of the
fevered young
who long for, wish and do.
The old are bawdy in their method
garish
they lean
outward for too long.
scared and dim.

Along the landings
he read about the success of the personal adverts
but it didn't cross his mind that she would come.
"They make them like that
heavy and ugly so you don't ask."
he said
explaining his club foot
"had it since birth, no one asks anymore so I don't say."
"my wife left me, they always do that,
go."
His lips shook
he was
the oldest man in the room
the collar tore at his neck.
Far later
He gave her the poem
saying "at least it'll make interesting scrap paper"
she looked down    avoided his foot.



Along the landings
Found himself looking out for her far and more than
once too often.

In Asda their trolleys crossed
no one asked
hung there
a while.
It was
An unhandled resistance    a difficult moment.



(2004-2005)

## Author's Note

*Along the landings* is a long poem based on my work as a social worker within a run-down post-war estate in south-east England. the landings are the walkways between the flats.

ER

Printed in the United Kingdom
by Lightning Source UK Ltd.
108048UKS00001B/122